view by Jim Walker

T̲o the volunteer members *who have made this museum possible during its thirty years of existence.*

Railway

ODYSSEY

A Guidebook to the
Orange Empire Railway
Museum, Perris, California

by Paul Hammond

FRONT COVER. Ventura County Railway No. 2, built in 1922 for use as a logging engine in the Pacific Northwest, ended its service career on a shortline running from Oxnard to Port Hueneme, in California. On its right, Pacific Electric Railway No. 1001 was one of the last all-wooden interurban cars constructed for the Pacific Electric, in 1913. It helped open P.E.'s new line to San Bernardino, in 1914, and thereafter spent its life roaming far and wide over the "World's Biggest Interurban."

BACK COVER. Los Angeles Railway No. 1201 was the first of 250 similar, all-steel cars built for the L.A. Ry. during 1921-1924. It poses here on the museum's "loop" line, a testimonial to the restoration skills of the museum's volunteer workers. In the lower photo, Ventura County Railway No. 2 is seen again on the "main line" at the museum, this time with a train of vintage Atchison, Topeka & Santa Fe and Union Pacific passenger cars.   **Three photos, Jim Walker**

FRONTISPIECE. *Silhouetted against cloudy skies, Ventura County steamer No. 2 was captured in this stunning view by Jim Walker, in 1982.*

RAILWAY ODYSSEY

ISBN 0-933563-06-X

ORANGE EMPIRE

Post Office Box 548
Perris, California 92370
Telephone (714) 657-2605

Railway Museum

First Edition: Summer 1987

Printed and Bound in the United States of America

Contents

Back when streetcars were a part of everyday life in Los Angeles, a stray camera caught Los Angeles Railway No. 1201 in the act of pulling around the streetcar loop at Los Angeles Union Station, with the Terminal Annex in the background. The year was 1946. In the lower photo, a long string of "reefers" (refrigerated boxcars) was headed eastbound at the summit of Cajon Pass in 1949. Freeways and faster-paced lifestyles would soon make for drastic changes to this less hurried way of life.

Above, J.N. Spencer; below, Stan Kistler

FOREWORD

CALIFORNIA was once served by an impressive array of public transportation. Steam, and later Diesel-powered trains carried freight and passengers to and from the Golden State, and also between dozens of cities throughout California.

In the cities, local streetcars carried commuters, shoppers, and school children to work, to the store, and to school. Suburban and commuter electric trains carried people to and from the suburbs, and interurban electric trains ran between some of the larger cities in our state.

A visit to the Orange Empire Railway Museum is a journey into the past — the recent past — for it was only yesterday that rail transportation was an important part of our lives. Welcome back to another era. We hope you enjoy your visit.

———◆•◆———

Against a classic Southern California backdrop of snow-covered peaks, Ventura County Railway No. 2 puffs her way through dormant fields, with AT&SFRy mail car No. 60 and combination baggage-passenger car No. 2602, and Soo Line Business Car No. 54 bringing up the rear. The date: March 27, 1982.

Mark Effle collection

PART ONE

Introduction

The Main Line Railroad Collection

SOUTHERN CALIFORNIA celebrated a landmark event in 1876 as the nation celebrated 100 years of freedom. The completion of the first rail link to Los Angeles that year was to change the landscape drastically in the coming years from a cattle-ranching expanse to a thriving agricultural area; ultimately to a series of spread-out metropolitan areas.

Silly as it may sound to us today, the railroad company at that time saw no future in Southern California; it was merely another place to build through on the way towards New Orleans from San Francisco. Had it not been for some diligent work by visionary city fathers, the Southern Pacific would have bypassed the Los Angeles Basin in favor of a shorter route through the Mojave desert!

Thus began the railroad era in Southern California history. Soon a second railway, the Atchison, Topeka & Santa Fe, entered Southern California, touching off the first of several land booms which brought thousands to the area to stay. New towns were founded; those already here grew in numbers and size. The stage was set for the rapid growth that was to follow.

Railroad building first began in the United States around 1830. It was not until the 1870s, however, that railroad lines were built to connect Southern California with the rest of the state and the nation. Consequently, the museum's collection of historic rail vehicles dates from the 1870s onward, as does the story it tells. Let's turn back the pages of history . . .

Chapter 1

Passenger Trains

A RIDE on the early steam railroads of Southern California usually meant a ride on a wooden day coach, often too hot or too cold, and dimly lit. But what a huge step forward it was, compared to the early stagecoaches and wagons.

During the 1870s and 80s, the passenger was expected to sleep in the not-too-comfortable coach seat, even on journeys lasting several days. Meals were gulped down at a lunch counter, while the train waited a short while at stops. Also, changing cars was not a safe proposition while the train was running, in these days of open platform cars; consequently one usually rode in the same car for much of the journey.

Railroad travel began to acquire more sophistication as time went by. The railroads, in fierce competition for passengers, turned to offering more speed, comfort, and luxury. During the 1890s and early 1900s, the railroads introduced famous name trains, such as the **California Limited, Sunset Limited, Golden State Limited**, and the **DeLuxe**. Passenger trains became showpieces with plush seats and inlaid wood. The dining car with snowy linens and impeccable service, sleeping car complete with the helpful porter and parlor-car service for daytime travel comfort were all introduced during this "golden era". And by now, enclosed vestibules (plat-

Southern California Classic. Look closely at the many details on this car. The stained glass in the arched windows, the fine hand-painted line-work on the car sides, and the wrought-iron grillwork around the back platform all combine to make for a classic of the carbuilder's art. Built by Pullman in 1910, the car had a steel frame sheathed in wood. *Turn to page 14 for more views of this car.*

Smithsonian collection

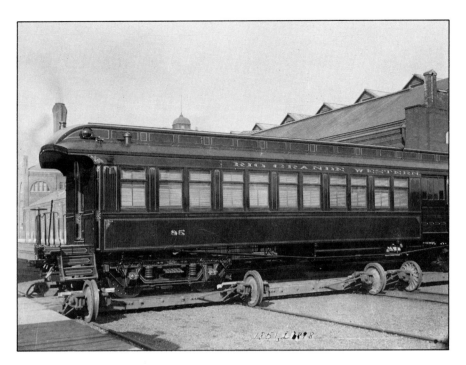

The interior of Rio Grande Western No. 95, left, originally sported fine varnished woodwork, hard wooden seats, and ornate gas lamps, while the exterior, above, showcased the painters' craftsmanship, all hand-painted on the car using a brush. Note the open vestibules (platforms) on the car. This kind of craftsmanship was typical of the period (the car was built in 1891 entirely of wood). This car later became Denver & Rio Grande Western No. 552; it was purchased for movie studio use and many years later was brought to the museum for display.
Smithsonian collection

forms) on the cars made it possible to walk, in comfort and safety, from one end of the train to the other. Each train became a "Hotel on Wheels". By this time (1920s) the cars used on trains had become stylishly plainer, although by no means less comfortable, and the all-steel "heavyweight" car had become standard (earlier cars were constructed of wood.)

Something new was introduced in late 1934: lightweight cars pulled by newly-designed Diesel and streamlined steam engines. The streamlined train was to the older, "heavyweight" trains what a 747 jetliner today is to an old, propeller-driven airplane — quite something! The gleaming new trains offered hope and optimism to a Depression-laden nation, and soon the names of the new trains were household words, synonymous with modernity and sophistication. The **Super Chief, City of Los Angeles**, and **Zephyr**, for example, were also famous due to numerous trips made by glamorous movie stars of the 30s and 40s. Lasting into the 50s and 60s, the "streamline" era was truly the high point in rail passenger travel.

Unfortunately, the automobile and the airplane eventually proved too great a challenge. By the 1960s, more and more famous trains were being discontinued. Finally Amtrak was established in 1971 to take over the remaining service.

The interior of Atchison, Topeka, & Santa Fe parlor-observation car No. 1204, above, shows how the Southern California mission-style motif was the prominent feature of the car's styling. This car is believed to have been built for use on excursion trains following the route of the "Kite-Shaped Track" through Fullerton, Riverside, San Bernardino, Redlands, Pasadena, and Los Angeles; it was also to see service on the Los Angeles-San Diego trains "Saint" and "Angel" in the 'teens. The car was built in 1910; it was refurbished and renumbered 3209 in the early 1920's and ended up its service as a bunkhouse for railroad work crews. As such, below, it was photographed in the 70's, its wood sides now sheathed in steel but a trace of its former glory still showing in the painted-over stained-glass window.

Above, Smithsonian collection; below, Orange Empire Railway Museum

Preserved "just as it was", Santa Fe Railway Post Office (RPO) Car No. 60, built in 1924, demonstrates the way the mail was distributed in the United States not too many years ago. Hundreds of similar cars operated on different railroads across the country, picking up, sorting enroute, and dropping off mail along the way, "Rain or Shine".

Jim Walker

(Previous Page) Silhouetted against Joshua Trees and tumbleweeds, Santa Fe's "California Limited" streaks through the Mojave Desert near Victorville, circa 1950, in this striking view of railroading — the way it was. When you really stop to think about it, not only is the museum preserving technology from previous generations, but also a way of life.

Donald Duke

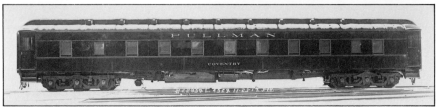

Pullman sleeping car "Corydon", opposite, top, originally had an interior paint finish that simulated wood paneling (the car was constructed almost entirely of steel). Built in 1917, the car was used in a "general service pool" which meant use on crack name trains, winter service to Florida, and western destinations in the summer. A sister car to Corydon, the "Coventry", is pictured opposite, below, to illustrate the original exterior appearance of the "Corydon". The original interior appearance of Santa Fe's "heavyweight" coaches, above, such as the No. 3010, built in 1927 almost entirely of steel, shows how the lavish decoration of earlier years had given way to a more austere and open look. The addition of air conditioning and removal of the upper window panes was to change the appearance of the car in later years.

All: Smithsonian collection

Santa Fe Horse Express Car No. 1999, left, was built in 1930 for special use in transporting prize racehorses to racetracks all over the country. As such, it was seen on occasion at the Santa Anita Racetrack in Baldwin Park.

B.A. Black

The northern section of Santa Fe Train No. 23, the "Grand Canyon Limited," rounds the horseshoe curve at Caliente, California, on its way downhill after having topped the summit of Tehachapi Pass. The diesel-electric locomotive is a relative newcomer at this date (1950) but already the steam locomotive is vanishing on Southern California trains. The coaches in this train are sisters to the type pictured on the previous page (interior view). Above, this photograph was taken during a "dinner train" put on by the museum in (1980) in an effort to raise funds. Union Pacific Lounge-Dormitory Car No. 1530, which was remodeled into a semi-streamlined car in 1954 from an older car, served as the "Diner" for the event.

**Left, Stan Kistler;
above, Jim Walker collection**

Another special event at the museum, "Union Pacific Day", found this trim freight train of (appropriately) Union Pacific freight cars behind Ventura County Railway steamer No. 2. The train is headed south towards the museum, approaching 11th Street in this 1982 view.

Jim Walker

Chapter 2

Freight Trains

THE COMPLETION of the first transcontinental railroad to Sacramento (1869) and the subsequent construction of the first rail connection to Southern California (1876) was to have a profound impact on the economy of all California. It was now possible to ship goods to and from the state, in large quantity, relatively quickly and cheaply. The importance of this cannot be underestimated, as the coming of the railroads was what changed California from an isolated gold mining and cattle ranching area to a thriving agricultural and manufacturing region.

———————◆•◆———————

Early Southern California freight trains brought goods of all sorts to the growing towns in the area — coal and wood for fuel, dry goods and general merchandise, whiskey for local saloons, and lumber to be used in the construction of fast-rising Victorian and Queen Anne style cottages and houses. The traditional boxcar and flatcar were used mainly in this service.

Soon the area was transformed into a booming agricultural area, growing grapes, nuts, and the famous citrus fruits, among other things.

Beginning in the 1880s, the "fruit express" train became an important part of Southern California at harvest time. Solid trains of "reefer" cars, as they were called, rushed perishables quickly to market in an ice-cooled environment.

Before the turn of the century, oil was discovered in the Los Angeles area, and soon the tank car had become an important part of Southern California railroading. Other types of cars were built to satisfy the special

(Opposite) The familiar boxcar comes in many shapes and sizes. The Santa Fe boxcar in the upper photo shows typical early wooden carbody construction; "truss rods" under the floor (between the wheelsets) support the load in this car, which was built in 1913 and had a capacity of 80,000 pounds. The Pacific Electric boxcar in the middle photo, built in 1924, had a steel frame which allowed it a higher capacity of 100,000 pounds. The lower photo shows one of the familiar "Pacific Fruit Express" refrigerator cars, which played such an important part in Southern California's agricultural growth. All-steel construction was the norm by the time (1937) this car was constructed.

Middle, Daryl Knapp; others, Jim Walker

(This page) One of the more unusual freight cars at the museum is this side-dump car, above, which was constructed in 1916 for mining service in Ajo, Arizona. Large air cylinders on the car are capable of dumping ore in either direction, rather forcefully! This timeless photo, below, was taken in 1953 at Slaton, Texas, as Santa Fe's Slaton-LaMesa mixed train did its daily duties in a way reminiscent of earlier times. "Mixed" meant that the train carried both freight and passengers; it also usually meant an unhurried ride with many stops along the way to pick up and drop off cars.

Above, Mark Effle, Daryl Knapp collection; below, Stan Kistler

Ventura County No. 2 and train passes "Oil Junction" on the way back towards the museum, silhouetted against cloudy skies. Union Pacific caboose 25129 is one of the more modern cars in the collection, built in 1944 to help out with the tremendous chore of moving goods and people for the war effort. Right, a sunny Southern California day finds Pacific Electric electric locomotive No. 1624 doing the honors in about the same location. The Pacific Electric was a major freight hauler in Southern California; even today much of the original P.E. right-of-way remains in service, although Southern Pacific diesel-electrics pull the trains these days.

Both, Jim Walker

needs of shippers, such as vinegar and wine tank cars, gravel and grain "hoppers", and livestock cars.

The railroads during WWI and WWII moved unprecedented quantities of goods, supplies, and ammunition to help the war effort. But after the Second World War, increased use of alternate forms of transport (trucking and air cargo) led to many changes in the railroad industry. Today the typical freight train of boxcars, tank cars, and flat cars can still be seen, but railroads now depend for much of their revenue on large shipments of coal and grain, and on intermodal forms of shipment such as containers and "piggyback" truck trailers.

Chapter 3

Cabooses and Work Equipment

THE CABOOSE has been a familiar sight on the tail end of freight trains in this country since the 1850s, when the first caboose was contrived, it is said, by rigging a shed on a flatcar for the brakeman and conductor to ride in. No less than thirteen cabooses have been preserved at Orange Empire, from early wood-bodied models right up to more modern all-steel ones.

Another important facet of railroading is work equipment, carried in special trains, to be on site for a specific task. Among these were wrecking trains, which were dispatched in a big hurry to pick up the pieces after a wreck. There were also special cars for foremen and workers, and sometimes their families, to stay in during major track construction or rebuilding projects. Equipment used in this type of service is generally referred to as "maintenance of way" equipment, abbreviated MW for short.

Southern Pacific *wooden caboose No. 570, built in 1924 in the S.P.'s own shops, was stopped at the south end of the museum's main line circa 1980 in this view.*

Richard A. Smith

Pacific Electric caboose No. 1962, built in 1939 at the P.E. Shops, was unusual in that it had no cupola or bay window from which to view the train. It is shown above near Gage Ave. along the P.E.'s "Four Tracks" in the mid 1950s. Santa Fe D918, built in 1929 in company shops, was a Drover's caboose, with accommodations for those accompanying livestock shipments on their way to market.

Above, Jim Walker; below, Norman Johnson

Santa Fe Foreman's Car No. 193673, above, began its career in 1904 as a furniture boxcar. It was converted into mobile living quarters for foremen and their families at an unknown date. Below, another example of maintenance-of-way equipment at the museum is this familiar human-powered handcar, used by track crews in days of old to "commute" to the workplace. This particular one was built in 1921 by the Buda Foundry & Manufacturing Co., of Harvey, Illinois.

Above, John LePrince; below, Daryl Knapp

Mojave Northern No. 2, shown pulling S.P. caboose No. 570, is known as a "saddle tanker", since it carries its fuel and water in tanks which wrap around the boiler. Built by Davenport in 1917, the engine spent most of its life in the Mojave Desert near Victorville.

Photographer unknown

Chapter 4

Locomotives

THE LOCOMOTIVES which were used to pull freight and passenger trains were, like the cars they pulled, of many different types.

Steam locomotives, which first ran in America in 1830, are still a fondly remembered part of American history. They were used on American railroads up into the 1950s and 60s, when the more efficient Diesel-electric locomotives took over the tasks formerly performed by their boiling brethren.

Small steam locomotives brought the first trains to California in the 1860s and 70s. At first these locomotives burned wood for fuel, but as the supply of wood near the tracks diminished, most western railroads converted to burning crude oil.

Different types of locomotives were used for freight and passenger service; the freight locomotives generally had smaller diameter driving wheels, for traction and power, while those used in passenger service had larger diameter driving wheels for speed.

The interurban electric railways in California also carried a fair amount of freight, with the trains being pulled by powerful electric locomotives.

Before the Diesel-electric locomotive came into wide use on main line railroads, there were many experiments with gasoline and distillate fuel engines. The Diesel engine eventually proved the clear leader for railway use. Ultimately, after many experiments with hydraulic and mechanical transmissions, an electric transmission was settled on as the most practical. The Diesel engine, directly connected to a generator, generates electricity, which in turn powers electric traction motors which are directly geared to the axles. In essence, the modern-day Diesel locomotive is an electric locomotive with a mobile Diesel generator riding along to provide the electricity!

Ventura County Railway No. 2 shown, left, near Port Hueneme (near Oxnard) where it was sent to help out with the war effort, started out in 1922 as Cascade Lumber Co. No. 107. Many modifications were made to the locomotive in later years. In the photograph on the opposite page, Southern Pacific No. 1474, a 1,000 hp diesel-electric switch engine built in 1952 by ALCO, helps dump ballast along the museum's main line in 1984.

Left, photographer unknown; right; Jim Walker

Above, United States Air Force No. 8580 was built in 1944 by General Electric. Sacramento Northern electric locomotive No. 653, built also by G.E. in 1928, opposite, is known as a "steeplecab" locomotive because the control cab is centered in the carbody. The famous "California Zephyr" streamliner stopped at this same station (Marysville) in the 1950s and 60s.

Jim Walker

PART TWO

Introduction

The Interurban and Street Railway Collection

FROM THE BEGINNING, the main focus of the electric railway collection at Orange Empire has been Southern California and its own uniquely-styled trolleys — the Pacific Electric, the Los Angeles Railway, and the San Diego Electric Railway. Over the years, however, the collection has grown to include examples from all over California: Bakersfield, Visalia, Fresno, San Francisco, the East Bay (Oakland, Berkeley, etc.), Marin County, and the Sacramento Valley. Add to this, for breadth and contrast, cars from Salt Lake City, Utah; Hutchinson, Kansas; New Orleans, Louisiana; Vancouver, Canada; Kyoto, Japan; and Dublin, Ireland; and the museum has a collection broad enough to tell the story of the electric trolley, and its impact on California in particular.

The museum's collection of electric railway vehicles includes all different types, from many different cities, even several which ran in other countries. Illustrating these differences, Los Angeles Railway No. 1201, in the foreground, spent its life on stop-and-go, local streetcar lines, while in the background, Pacific Electric No. 498 was built originally for Southern Pacific's electrified suburban lines in the East Bay cities of Oakland, Alameda, and Berkeley, coming south during WWII to transport shipyard workers to San Pedro. In its later years, this car was often seen on Pacific Electric CATALINA SPECIAL trains operating to the front door of the Great White Steamship Terminal in Wilmington. One of the less obvious differences between these two cars is to be found by looking at the rails in the foreground; the L.A. Ry. ran on narrow-gage trackage, which is to say that the distance between the rails was less than the standard U.S. track gage of 4 feet 8½ inches. The museum is the only one of many similar in the U.S. to have this dual-gage operation.

Jim Walker

Early "streetcars", such as this one pausing at the Florence Hotel in San Diego circa 1885, were powered by horses. Average speed for a horsecar was 4-5 miles an hour, little more than walking speed.

San Diego Historical Society — Ticor collection

Chapter 5

Early Local Transportation

IN THE EARLY to mid-1800s, Southern California business activity was centered around the downtown areas of Los Angeles and San Diego. These served as the hubs of activity for their respective areas, being the bases for shipping (by mule teams before the advent of the railroads), supply, and trading. In those pre-transit days the average man rode to town by horse or walked, and those living in the towns got around largely by walking.

The populations of the small communities in Southern California, as well as the two major cities, grew rapidly after the advent of the railroads. The growth of these communities was limited, though, by the primitive local transportation available — people would only walk so far to get downtown. Some form of urban transit was needed.

The first such service began in 1827, in New York, when horse-drawn stagecoaches began operating. Roads at the time were often paved with mud, however, and the solution was not long in coming: America's first street railway was incorporated in 1831, also in New York, the idea being that a horse could pull a more heavily loaded stage, in all kinds of weather, if the stage were placed on rails. The line was a success, but it wasn't until the 1850s, when the United States had a half-dozen cities of more than 100,000 population, that street railway building began in earnest.

Insofar as Southern California was concerned, it wasn't until the mid-1880s that the first horsecar lines were introduced. Several of the larger towns, such as Pasadena, Riverside, Ontario, and Santa Monica, as well as Los Angeles and San Diego, were blessed with these marvelous vehicles — which could do six miles per hour or better!

Horsecars were a tremendous improvement over walking. But, even the horses could only walk so far, and they were expensive to care for, feed, and clean up after.

Steam locomotives could have pulled small passenger cars. However, they suffered from several major drawbacks. They frightened horses, offended residents with their noise and exhaust, and the small size necessary for street use made them relatively inefficient. Because of this, "Steam Dummies", as street locomotives were called, were usually limited to suburban use. Redlands, San Bernardino, Los Angeles, and San Diego all saw the steam dummy come and go.

There were also attempts nationwide to operate cars with engines propelled by ammonia gas, soda, naptha, and compressed air. Within the more limited technology of the day, the efforts were all failures — the devices having a tendency to either blow up, fizzle, or be economically impractical.

A promising development came in 1873, with the appearance of cable cars. Their increased speed (as much as 11 miles an hour!) made them tremendously popular. For a short while, the cable car appeared to be the solution to the urban transportation problem. The major drawback was the cost of such a system: a huge investment was required in the construction of special trackwork to carry the cars and the cable which pulled them, the powerhouse which propelled the cable, and the cable itself, which was often several miles long. As a result, only the largest of cities ever saw cable cars, such as New York, Kansas City, Seattle, Chicago, and of course San Francisco. In Southern California, only Los Angeles and San Diego ever had them. The cable car boom ended quickly; today the cars survive only in the city of their birth, San Francisco, as a National Historic Landmark.

California Street Cable Railroad No. 53, a sister to the museum's No. 43, was changing ends at the corner of Jones and O'Farrell in the mid-1950's. Market Street, San Francisco's main thoroughfare, is in the left background. Similar cars still run in The City.

Interurban Press collection

This ad appeared in the 1889 book by Fred H. Whipple entitled The Electric Railway (a reprint of which is available from the museum). One look at the size of typical 1880s batteries, though, and it is easy to see why the battery-powered streetcar did not come into general usage.

Orange Empire Railway Museum

San Francisco Municipal Railway No. 171 was headed out the "M" line towards Ocean View in the late 1950's, and had stopped for a moment at the West Portal of Twin Peaks Tunnel. In San Francisco as elsewhere, streetcars played a major role in opening up outlying areas for development, areas which had previously been shunned because of the time it would take to travel downtown by horseback or newfangled automobile. The electric railway was truly a marvelous development for its time.

A.M. Payne

Chapter 6

The Electric Railway

BY THE 1880s, it had become obvious to the more practical of innovators that electricity was the permanent answer to the street railway's motive power problem. In 1881 the world's first commercial electric railway was opened, near Berlin, Germany. The electric railway industry was making a promising start by 1888, when there were 21 companies operating 172 electric cars over 86 miles of track in this country.

It was at this time that Frank J. Sprague, the "Father of Electric Traction", came on the scene. Sprague first came up with an improved method of mounting the electric motors; earlier installations had tended to shake the cars to pieces. His most important contribution to the budding technology was the invention of "multiple-unit control", whereby several cars coupled together could be operated, each under their own power, by one man from a single set of controls. This was important because it made electrification of elevated lines, subways, and suburban railways practical, where long trains were necessary for rush-hour crowds, as opposed to the single cars usually seen in local streetcar service.

Since that time, there's been nothing quite like the electric trolley car in the history of North America. Its impact on domestic life was swift and stupendous. In the 30 years before 1917, almost nothing stood in its way. Without the electric trolley, urban life on this continent hardly seemed worth living. From the largest city to the smallest town, communities struggled mightily to get services started and, once they had begun, moved heaven and earth to get them improved and extended. Why? Because in that pre-auto age the installation of an electric

Kyoto, Japan city streetcar No. 19, built in the 1890's mostly of wood, may seem a long way from home, but this car is typical of many similar ones which ran in cities all over the U.S. before the turn of the century, including Los Angeles. The car was retired from active service in 1961 and placed at the museum by Mr. Philip Goldman. No. 19 was actually constructed in the U.S. and shipped in "kit" form to Japan for assembly.

Jim Walker

trolley system within a community overnight made the movement of large numbers over short distances not just possible for the first time in man's history but utterly simple and cheap. The coming of the electric trolley opened up possibilities for the amelioration of overcrowded conditions and an enrichment of urban life for the masses that then seemed limitless.

These, after all, were the days when North America had finally turned its back on the frontier, seeing its future lying instead with the rapidly growing cities and their industries. Many felt civilized life to be possible only in urban areas, and it was the trolley companies in seemingly casual fashion which emphasized that point of view as they became agents of the city growth (largely unplanned) in and around the areas they served.

By 1900 (some would argue even before that date) the trolley had become a robust and reliable machine of docile men, as even the most casual observer could not fail to see. One man, with a twirl of his wrist, could start, stop and vary the speed with an ease utterly unknown to any other form of animal or mechanical traction, and he could do it without compromising anyone's safety.

It was not long, therefore, before the trolley sped beyond the city and its suburbs. In those pre-auto days, few roads were adequate for sustained all-weather use, and short-distance travel from most farms or villages to a railhead, county seat or city, could be fraught with difficulty. Interstate links by rail and water were well developed by this time, but short distance intrastate transport was not. It was the electric trolley which held out promise of solving this problem. At the turn of the century, with the city trolley seemingly perfected, electric rail lines suddenly leaped beyond city cimits to connect whole strings of small or medium-sized towns with a county seat or a big town.

The interurbans (as they quickly became known) could provide fast, clean, electric passenger service over distances and through areas the steam railroads either could not or would not cover. They also could provide quick same-day freight service for less-than-carload perishables, and the economic stimulus given rural areas by the coming of an interurban was very real.*

---

* Quoted with permission from **Trolley to the Past,** Interurban Press, 1983.

Bakersfield and Kern Electric Railway No. 4, beautifully restored at the museum, was photographed early in the century at the Bakersfield depot of the Santa Fe Railway. The body configuration is known as a "California Car", since only in the Golden State was the climate pleasant enough for outdoor riding year-'round. This car was "born with the century", in 1900. For more views of this car, please turn to pages 86-87.

Joseph F. Webber collection

Hill of Howth Tramway No. 2, a double-deck Irish tram built in 1901, operated until 1959 on a short suburban line near Dublin. It found its way to Southern California aboard a cargo ship. Opposite, British Columbia Electric Railway No. 1225, built in St. Louis, Mo., in 1913, ran in interurban service in the Vancouver area. It is representative of hundreds of cars which once ran in interurban service (between towns and cities) all over the midwestern U.S. Being constructed of both wood and steel, No. 1225 is known as a "composite" car.

Above, Orange Empire Railway Museum; opposite, Dick Smith

The largest intercity electric system in the United States was Southern California's own **Pacific Electric**, which began in 1895 with a line from downtown Los Angeles to Pasadena, while the longest intercity electric run was found on Northern California's **Sacramento Northern**, running between San Francisco, Oakland, Sacramento, and Chico.

A third type of electric railway was also quite prevalent in California: the suburban (commuter) electric railway. A functional cross between the local streetcar and the interurban, the suburban electric railway combined fast running with many stops. This type of railway line usually began at either a large downtown station or ferryboat terminal, and ran to the suburbs from that point with frequent stops being made. Much of the large Pacific Electric system in Southern California can be placed into this category. (The P.E. actually was a combination of all three types: local, suburban and interurban).

As the century turned, the boom was on. The electric railway industry mushroomed in size until by 1920 it was the fifth largest industry in size in the U.S., a fact that seems incredible today. City populations doubled; suburbs sprang up. In 1890 street railways carried two billion passengers; in 1982, five billion which was more than several times the number carried on the nation's steam railroads.

The decline and lingering death of the electric railway industry began as early as World War I, when rising costs plunged many companies into insolvency. In the 1920s the use of the private auto and rapid spread of the paved highway network caused transit riding to drop off and as a defensive

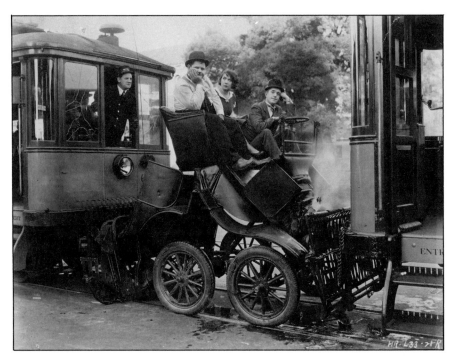

Laurel and Hardy, *famous comedy duo of the 1920s and 30s, have gotten themselves into "another fine mess", opposite, above, sandwiched between streetcars of the Los Angeles Railway. Both the Pacific Electric and the L.A. Ry. were convenient props for the nearby film capital of Hollywood. Below, Los Angeles Railway No. 665, a "Huntington Standard" city streetcar designed by streetcar magnate Henry E. Huntington (of Huntington Library, Beach, and Drive fame) was crafted mostly of wood in 1911. This was the type of car that Los Angeles grew up with; at one time, there were 747 of them roaming the streets of L.A. The wraparound window was an elegant, distinctly unique Southern California touch. Above, this L.A. street scene taken in 1948 shows streetcars, Acme traffic signals, and traffic congestion — all blanketed in the infamous L.A. smog.*

Opposite, above, Ralph Cantos collection; below, Jim Walker; above, A.M. Payne

Speeding over a high trestle through Balboa Park in March 1949, San Diego Electric Railway No. 528, a modern PCC city car built in 1938, had only a few more months left to run before buses would take over. On the opposite page, above, a prominent Baptist minister was standing in the doorway of San Diego Electric Railway No. 152, a sister to Orange Empire's No. 167, on Broadway in San Diego. The Spreckels Building is in the background. Below, the interior of the enclosed section of this car. Constructed in 1915, these cars were built for the Exposition held in San Diego that same year. One end of the cars was open; the other enclosed.

Above, A.M. Payne; opposite, both, Lyle Judd

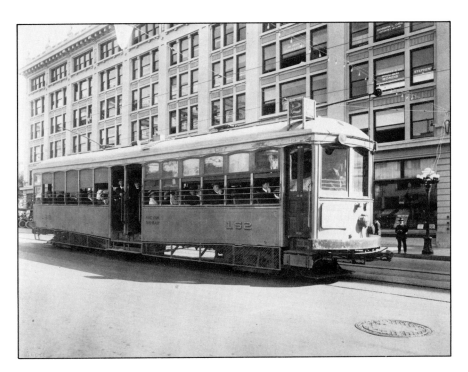

The **"World's Biggest Interurban"** was the title given to the Pacific Electric during the 1920's. And it truly was, with over 1,000 miles of lines; hundreds of streetcars, suburban cars, and interurban cars; and over one thousand departures daily from Los Angeles. Above, P.E. No. 1001, a classic of the carbuilder's art in wood, was built in 1913. A tragic wreck at Vineyard (in West L.A.) that same year, involving wooden cars which splintered on impact, resulted in No. 1001 and her sisters being the last wooden cars built for the Pacific Electric. These cars opened service on the long interurban line to San Bernardino in 1914. Opposite, above, P.E. No. 331 was a "Birney Safety Car", built in 1918 to a standard design which was supposed to help cut labor and power consumption costs. The public disliked the bouncy and jerky ride on these cars; in spite of this, No. 331 rolled off many a mile on local lines in Long Beach, Pasadena, and the Inland Empire. Below, "Hollywood" car No. 717 was so named because it and its 159 sisters spent many years rolling along the streets of the Film Capital. In later years these cars saw service all over the P.E., and No. 717 ended its service career on the Watts local line in 1959.

All: Jim Walker

Riding along the lower deck of the San Francisco-Oakland Bay Bridge, Key System Transit Lines No. 179, a sister to OERM's No. 167, has the tracks all to itself circa 1955. The Key System was a suburban commuter line which connected the East Bay cities with San Francisco. Opposite, the three views each show the same car, at different stages during its service career. Built in 1930, it began it's service in Northern California, running between Sausalito, Mill Valley, and San Rafael on the Northwestern Pacific. As such, it was photographed, top, at San Anselmo in the mid-1930s. Note the absence of a trolley pole: the NWP used an electrified third rail for power distribution. During WWII, the car came south to help out with the war effort, transporting shipyard workers to and from Terminal Island, and the middle photo shows it as it appeared in this service, at Watts in 1946. After the war, the Pacific Electric refurbished the car, inside and out, for service to Santa Ana, Bellflower, and Long Beach. The bottom photo shows the car as it appeared in 1956; the 6th and Main Sts. Station (Los Angeles) is in the background. At one time, more than 1700 trains of the Pacific Electric visited this station daily.

Above, Jim Walker, opposite, above and middle, Warren K. Miller, opposite, below, Jim Walker

(Previous page) Market Street, San Francisco, in the late 1950's. Look at all those trolley buses and streetcars! At one time, Market Street had the heaviest streetcar traffic in the world, with four tracks which were jammed at rush hour. The museum has preserved several streetcars and trolley buses from San Francisco, including ones similar to those pictured.

San Francisco Public Utilities Commission, Jim Walker Collection

Fresno Traction No. 51, so ugly that it must have been designed by a committee, was built in 1913 at the height of the "hobbleskirt" craze. Milady could get on and off with just one dainty step. Fashions changed, however, and the streetcar company was left with a slow and ungainly car which was impossible to modernize. Below, New Orleans Public Service No. 913, built in 1923 by the Perley A. Thomas Co., is similar to the car featured in Tennessee William's play "A Streetcar Named Desire". Cars similar to this one still operate in the Crescent City.

Above, Bert Ward collection; below, O.A. Goessl

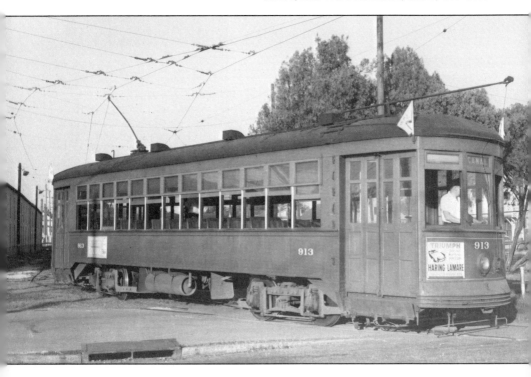

Los Angeles Railway No. 3001 was the first of 60 PCC streamliners delivered in 1937 to usher in a new era of quiet and comfortable transportation. Child actress Shirley Temple and L.A. Mayor Shaw had the honors of unveiling the revolutionary new car to the citizens of Los Angeles. By this time, motor and private autos were in fierce competition for passengers, and this car was the street railway industry's answer. The Los Angeles Railway and its successors would ultimately operate 165 cars of this design.

Arrow Studio, Ralph Cantos collection

measure, many lines eliminated conductors and went to one-man crews. New cars were bought to attract patronage; their generally lighter weight helped save on power usage and track wear. Lightly patronized rail lines were converted to bus operation. Never had a major industry had such a brief day in the sun.

World War II allowed a brief respite from the trend away from public transportation; gas and tire rationing again filled the trolleys and buses. In 1936, the industry even came up with a radically new, silent, streamlined streetcar, but it saved only the heavier rail lines in the bigger cities, and only for a few years at that.

Chapter 7

Special Cars and Work Equipment

BY 1900, the electric trolley was an accepted part of daily life. Besides carrying people to and from work, it collected freight, delivered packages, picked up fresh fruit and milk from the farmer for shipment to city markets, delivered mail, took people on pleasure trips, carried them to the hospital in ambulance cars, and to the grave in funeral cars.

Specialized cars were required for such services. Often they were simply older cars converted to a different configuration; just as often they were built new by a commercial builder, sometimes even by the railway company itself.

Many a steam railroad had one or more officers' cars, deluxe passenger cars in which the officials of the company could travel about their executive rounds. Few electric railway companies could afford this luxury; only the grandest or largest operations (of which there were a couple in California) had their own officers' cars.

Other specialized cars, known as "non revenue" cars, were required by electric railway companies for work duties. The tracks, the overhead wires, and the revenue fleet of cars required routine maintenance, and special cars were built to help crews perform these tasks as well as many others. Once again, the cars used in this service were converted from older cars or built new for these special duties.

Running on 7th near Spring St. in downtown L.A., Los Angeles Transit Lines No. 9225, a self-propelled 5-ton derrick, was built in L.A. Ry. company shops in 1912. (The Los Angeles Transit Lines succeeded the L.A. Ry. in 1944.)

Jim Walker

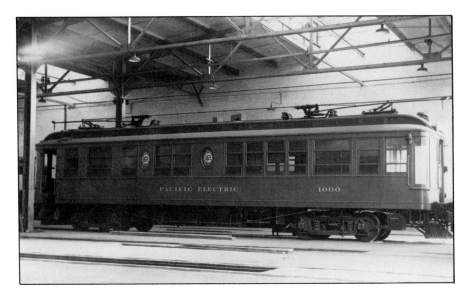

Pacific Electric No. 1000, above, was built in 1913 as part of the same order as car 1001 (see page 54). Shortly thereafter, the car was rebuilt into a "Private Car" for use by the company's top management. In the late 1930s, the car, known as the "Commodore", made a daily round trip to Balboa, where P.E. president Oscar A. Smith maintained a summer home. Note the stained glass in the oval windows. Below, P.E. line car 00157, built in 1915, was used for maintenance of the overhead wire. The wires could be worked on while live, since the car was built of wood.

Above, Lorin Silleman, below Norman K. Johnson

Los Angeles Railway No. 9310 is a rail grinder, sent around to grind the rails back to smoothness; particularly at car stops corrugations would develop. The 9310's passage in the wee hours of the night was anything but inconspicuous, what with all the noise and the showers of sparks. Funeral streetcar "Descanso", below, from the Los Angeles Railway, offered a last trip in style for the dearly departed of the early 1900s. There was space for the coffin, and the mourners rode in a little chapel-like compartment. The car was later used as a clubhouse for railfans, atop Cajon Pass, before being brought to the museum in 1967.

Above, A.M. Payne, below, Jim Walker collection

PART THREE

About the Museum . . .

Chapter 8

Organization History

TODAY's Orange Empire Railway Museum was formed in 1975 by the merger of two predecessor groups, the Orange Empire Trolley Museum and the California Southern Railroad Museum. These two groups dated back to March of 1956 and December of 1955 respectively.

The two groups were originally founded for different purposes: one group wanted to preserve examples of electric traction, the other wanted to preserve steam railroad history. In the end, however, it was decided that a merger of the two would be in the best interests of historic preservation.

The museum is today the largest railway museum in the western United States, with over 1000 members; membership is open to all interested persons (inquire at the museum bookstore, or request an application at P.O. Box 548, Perris, CA 92370-0548.) Orange Empire Railway Museum is recognized as a non-profit, educational organization, and donations are tax deductible. Any contribution you can make will be appreciated; as you can imagine, the costs of building and maintaining this museum are phenomenal.

Travel Town, Los Angeles, 1956. Four of the museum's founding members posed for this photo, surrounded by cars which would be moved to Perris when the museum site was found in 1958. Time has proven that those guys really weren't crazy, going off and starting a railway museum! Below, the first car to arrive at the museum in 1958 was L.A.T.L. flatcar 9614. It sits here, forlornly, in a VERY empty field.

Above, Norman K. Johnson, below, Jim Walker

1960. More cars arrive. The rickety track was extended as the collection grew. The old farmhouse is in the background; this area today is the location of Broadway. Below, the "main line" at the museum in the mid 1960s was what today is the southern part of the "loop" line. A diesel generator grudgingly provided power for limited operations.

Both, Jim Walker

The north side of the loop takes shape, in 1966. This area is quite different in appearance today, with carbarns off to the left side of the tracks. Below, the first carbarn rises, in 1969, as Los Angeles Railway No. 525 passes by with a load of visitors.

Both, Jim Walker

The bookstore station building takes shape in 1968. Previous to this time, a small 4 by 8 foot building was the bookstore. Until 1973, below, the "loop" line at the museum wasn't really a loop. Loop cars took passengers around to the main line platform, then had to go all the way backwards around the loop, back to the bookstore. L.A. Ry. No. 525 and P.E. No. 717 illustrate the transfer procedure.

Above, Jim Walker, below, Tom Gray

Over the years, the tracks were extended as time, finances, and track materials allowed. Opening day for the museum's new "Northern Extension" back in 1977 prompted this occasion just above "Oil Junction" on the main line. Gliding south on today's main line, below, past the "pie" yard, P.E. No. 717 illustrates what time, money, dedication, and perseverance have accomplished at Orange Empire.

Both, Jim Walker

A strange place to find a streetcar? Not really, even though we must agree that it is not in its natural habitat, the city. This was Los Angeles Railway No. 665, on the back lot at a movie studio, being readied for moving to the museum in 1967. After being retired, streetcar bodies could be found performing a variety of duties, such as becoming sheds, lean-tos, even living rooms and kitchens for many Southern California homes!

Jim Walker

Chapter 9

From An Empty Field

WHERE did it all come from and how did it get here?

This question is asked by many of our visitors as they look around at the cars, tracks, and wires. Here are some answers.

Many of the cars were purchased at scrap prices from their former owners or scrap dealers. Occasionally, a few cars were donated either by generous individuals or railroad companies, to which many thanks are due.

It was necessary in most cases to load the cars onto lowbed trailers, for a long highway trip to Perris, (many trips were made before the advent of freeways, as well) after which they had to be unloaded, usually by means of a hastily-constructed ramp. Once in a while, it was possible to ship a car to the museum via the railroad (on its own wheels or on a flatcar) but this simply was not practical in most cases. And for some time there was no rail connection to the museum; cars which came this way had to be brought from Perris down to the museum by "snap track", a painfully slow task.

All the tracks around the museum (and there are over three miles of them) were taken up from donated rail sidings all over Southern California, then trucked out to the museum to be relaid. Many of the special street switches were removed from streets and storage yards once used by the **Los Angeles Railway** and the **Pacific Electric.** The poles to hold up the wire came, again, from all over Southern California, often from these same railway systems.

Even many of the buildings have been moved to the museum from various locations, after having been taken apart for shipment. The list of where it all came from and how it got here is endless and fascinating.

San Francisco Municipal Railway No. 162 is "GOING TO THE . . . TROLLEY MUSEUM", via low-bed trailer from the Bay Area. There weren't many freeways in 1958, either!

Jim Walker

This site in 1958 was virtually empty. Nothing was here to greet the first members except the small rock house dating back to the settlement of Pinacate, and the old farmhouse nearby.

Since that time, the progress has been phenomenal. Most amazing is the fact that its all accompished by volunteers. Yes, dedicated individuals who donate their labor and talents freely, in their spare time. For them, this is truly a "labor of love".

The money to make the museum go and grow comes mainly from donations by members and visitors, and from revenues of the bookstore, railway operations, special publications, and special events.

From an empty field . . . to the museum it is today.

Soo Line business car No. 54 arrives at the museum on its own wheels, in 1974. Unfortunately, most cars in the museum's collection could not be brought to Perris in this manner, due to problems such as different track gage, age, condition, etc. Below, Upland, 1977 — illustrating the museum's track-gathering methods.

Above, Jim Walker, below, Jeff Butler

Orange Empire Railway Museum collection

Sowbelly Saga

Los Angeles Railway "Sowbelly" No. 936, built in 1914, succumbed early on to the pressures of automobile competition. Retired in 1945, it was used, left, as a house in Baldwin Park. It was brought to the museum in 1979, with flowery wallpaper on the sides leftover from its dwelling days. Below, reunited with wheels in 1983, the car was pushed under cover by a tired yet triumphant crew.

All, Jim Walker

THE LOCAL HISTORY

Pinacate and Perris

THE CALIFORNIA SOUTHERN RAILWAY, building northward from San Diego Bay towards San Bernardino to meet the Santa Fe Railway, passed by the present day museum site in April of 1882. A station consisting of a box car on a rail siding was built to serve the settlement located here, known as Pinacate (Spanish for "stink bug") which was the supply center for local gold mines. One of the original buildings from this settlement remains today, in the picnic area behind the bookstore.

COUNTY OF
RIVERSIDE
HISTORICAL MARKER
NO. 053

PINACATE

THE TOWN OF PINACATE, NAMED FOR THE SURROUNDING MINING DISTRICT, BEGAN HERE IN 1882 ON THE NEW CALIFORNIA SOUTHERN RAILROAD. WHEN THE LAND TITLE BECAME CLOUDED, THE RAILROAD MOVED THE SIDING TWO MILES NORTH AMONG NEW AGRICULTURAL SETTLERS, STARTING THE TOWN OF PERRIS IN 1885. PINACATE FADED AWAY, BUT TWO BUILDINGS REMAINED WHEN THE ORANGE EMPIRE RAILWAY MUSEUM TOOK OVER THE SITE IN 1958.

This old rock house once served as the Post Office for Piñacate; the farmhouse in the background was reportedly a saloon.
All, Jim Walker

The Perris depot, located in downtown Perris on 4th Street. The Perris Valley Historical and Museum Association displays many interesting items inside.

Joe Garnard

In 1885, a dispute occurred between the railroad and local landowners. The depot was relocated about a mile north of the original site and renamed Perris, in honor of Fred T. Perris, who was chief engineer of the California Southern at that time. Perris became a junction point for branch lines to Lakeview, Hemet and San Jacinto. At this time, a wood frame building served as the Perris depot, but the citizens wanted a better building, and construction began on the Victorian-era station building which still stands in downtown Perris.

By the time the new station was completed (in 1891) disastrous floods in Temecula Canyon, thirty miles south of the museum, had permanently severed the through line to San Diego. So the grand building of brick and gingerbread ended up as a branch-line station, and the Santa Fe Railway (by now owner of the Cal Southern) built around the break by way of today's surf route between San Diego and Los Angeles.

In 1927, the railroad was abandoned southward from Perris to Elsinore when construction began on a dam ten miles south of the museum. The tracks between Perris and the museum lay unused for many years, finally being torn up for scrap during the early 1950s.

The Perris station was presented to the museum by the Santa Fe Railway in 1971. It remains a classic example of railroad station architecture of the late nineteenth century.

Conductor Bill Hatrick, properly attired for his duties, punches the ticket of an intrigued guest. This is a "living museum", where the visitor can actually ride the exhibits and get a feel for the transport modes of the past — and we think that's something extra special. We hope you do, too.

Alan Weeks

Chapter 10

Tomorrow

THE FUTURE of the museum is bright. Carbarns continue to rise, housing the historic collection for generations to come, along with other facilities for restoration, maintenance, and exhibition of the rail vehicles and related displays. The trackage on the museum's demonstration railway lengthens from year to year, as do the overhead wires.

Progress on the surface is slow, most of the work being accomplished on weekends and holidays by the volunteer membership. But the museum continually strives toward the day when it will truly offer the visitor a journey into another era of forgotten technology, and the scholar and historian the necessary research tools to understand and document this era. An ambitious master plan, which will take many years to complete, is now being implemented.

For the present, though, the way this museum is presented to you, the visitor, remains unique among museums. The function of the trolleys and trains at this museum was to move people. In order to recreate the full impact, in order to bring the history to life for future generatons, the cars and trains had to run, and they had to run in surroundings similar to those in which they once ran.

This is a unique historical display. We hope that your visit has heightened your interest in this amazing form of land transportation, and the era in which it was so significant. Tell your friends about us, and, say, why don't you come back and see us again sometime?

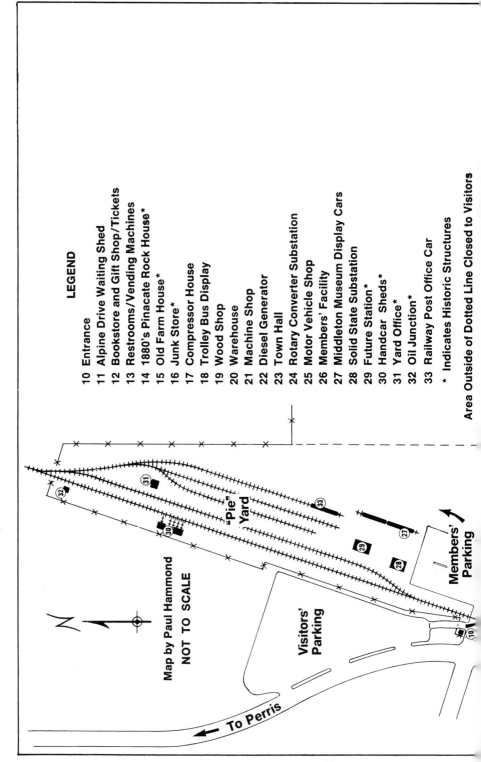

LEGEND

10 Entrance
11 Alpine Drive Waiting Shed
12 Bookstore and Gift Shop/Tickets
13 Restrooms/Vending Machines
14 1880's Pinacate Rock House*
15 Old Farm House*
16 Junk Store*
17 Compressor House
18 Trolley Bus Display
19 Wood Shop
20 Warehouse
21 Machine Shop
22 Diesel Generator
23 Town Hall
24 Rotary Converter Substation
25 Motor Vehicle Shop
26 Members' Facility
27 Middleton Museum Display Cars
28 Solid State Substation
29 Future Station*
30 Handcar Sheds*
31 Yard Office*
32 Oil Junction*
33 Railway Post Office Car

* Indicates Historic Structures

Area Outside of Dotted Line Closed to Visitors

Map by Paul Hammond
NOT TO SCALE

N

"Pie" Yard

Visitors' Parking

Members' Parking

To Perris

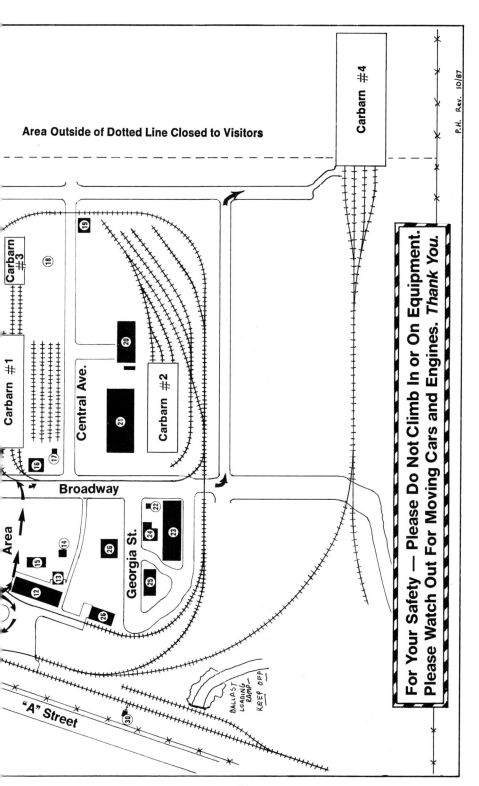

Area Outside of Dotted Line Closed to Visitors

Carbarn #4

Carbarn #3

Carbarn #1

Central Ave.

Carbarn #2

Broadway

Area

Georgia St.

BALLAST LOADING RAMP — KEEP OFF

"A" Street

For Your Safety — Please Do Not Climb In or On Equipment.
Please Watch Out For Moving Cars and Engines. *Thank You.*

P.H. Rev. 10/87

81

During 1980, the "main line" at the museum was extended northward an additional ½ mile. In the photo above, the first part of this trackage, headed towards town, was being rebuilt. Southern Pacific No. 1802, which has since been repainted as SP 1474, below, approaches 11th Street in Perris headed south towards the museum. The museum plans more extensions of the overhead wire and track reconstruction, northward on the main line, in the next few years.

Above, Jim Walker, below, Jeff Butler

Finishing touches are put on the museum's third carbarn, in 1983. Below, the museum's fourth carbarn, named in honor of longtime member Hugh T. Smith, rises. An ambitious master plan at the museum calls for additional carbarns and work areas to be built as time and money permit.

Both, Jim Walker

Filming for the movie "The Winds of War" at night at the museum. The museum is used occasionally for movie and commercial filming, when that "railroad" touch is desired.

Jim Walker

Shop Facilities

Two different shop facilities at the museum. Above, the inside of the machine shop, first phase of the planned "Sylvester Shops" where cars will be rebuilt and maintained. Until additional phases are built, however, makeshift "shop" facilities are often resorted to for big projects. The tender for Ventura County steamer No. 2 was being rebuilt at "Pepper Tree Shops", left, in this 1981 view.

Both, Jim Walker

The Rebuilding of a Streetcar

Before . . .

When it first made an appearance at the museum, Bakersfield & Kern Electric Railway No. 4 was in very poor and dilapidated condition.

Jim Walker

After being completely disassembled, the slow process of rebuilding the car began. The main frame and sides take shape.

Jim Walker

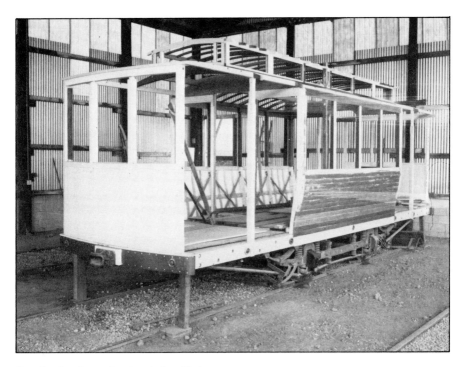

Framing for the roof and ends is added.

After ! ! !

The ten-year restoration of B&K No. 4 is finally completed in June of 1983. Joe and Norma Webber, dedicated husband and wife team who undertook the job, stand beside the sparkling car.

Sorry Eyed . . .

to Starry Eyed.

Another stunning example of what restoration can do for a car's disposition is evident in these before and after views of Los Angeles Railway No. 1201. The restoration took over five years to complete, but the results were well worth it.

Both, Jim Walker

There's something special about an old time streetcar ride . . .
Jim Walker

. . . and the volunteers who work on the cars, too!
Jim Walker

Roster of Preserved Railway Equipment

HORSE CARS:

No.	Co.	Type	Date	Builder	Length	Weight	Seats	Motors No.	Motors HP	Remarks
2(?)	?	DE ST ArRf Closed	c1875	B&W	15-5			N/A		Reputed once used in Pasadena
?	?	DE ST BbRf Closed	c1880	Stephenson	14-2			N/A		Std. gauge, on 42" gauge truck

CABLE CARS (3'6" [NARROW] GAUGE)

No.	Co.	Type	Date	Builder	Length	Weight	Seats	Motors No.	Motors HP	Remarks
43	CSCRR	DE DT DkRf California Style	c1907	CSCRR	30-5	11,500	34	N/A		

ELECTRIC CITY STREETCARS (3'6" [NARROW] GAUGE):

No.	Co.	Type	Date	Builder	Length	Weight	Seats	Motors No.	Motors HP	Remarks
Descanso	LARy	DE DT RRRf Funeral Car	1909	LARy	39-2	35,000	40			motors removed by LARy
7	LARy	DE DT DkRf California Style	1895	St Louis	35-5	42,000				body only, placed on trucks
19	Kyoto	DE ST DkRf Closed	c1898		27-8	18,200	40	2		from Kyoto, Japan
151	LARy	DE DT DkRf California Style	1898	St Louis	44-7	36,890	44	2		
525	LARy	DE DT DkRf California Style	1906	St Louis	44-7	43,000	44	4	35	
665	LARy	DE DT DkRf California Style	1911	St Louis	44-7	37,500	48	2	50	
744	LARy	DE DT DkRf California Style	1911	St Louis	44-7					body only
807	LARy	DE DT DkRf California Style	1911	St Louis	44-7					body only
936	LARy	DE DT DkRf Center Entrance	1914	St Louis	46-7	39,500				body only
1003	LARy	DE ST ArRf Birney	1920	American	28-0	16,760				body only
1160	LATL	DE DT ArRf California Style	1923	LARy	48-0	43,416	52	4	55	reblt from car blt in 1899
1201	LARy	DE DT ArRf California Style	1921	St Louis	48-0	44,500	48	4	40	
1423	LATL	DE DT ArRf Closed	1924	St Louis	48-0	47,000	48	4	40	
1450	LATL	DE DT ArRf Closed	1924	St Louis	48-0	46,280	48	4	40	
1559	LARy	DE DT ArRf California Style	1925	LARy	48-0	42,700	48	4	40	
2601	LATL	DE DT ArRf Closed, Peter Witt	1930	St Louis	49-0	44,580	55	4	50	
3001	LARy	SE DT ArRf PCC	1937	St Louis	46-0	34,780	61	4	55	
3100	LATL	SE DT ArRf PCC	1943	St Louis	46-0	34,240	61	4	55	
3165	LAMTA	SE DT ArRf PCC	1948	St Louis	46-5	37,600	58	4	55	

ELECTRIC CITY STREETCARS (4'8½" [STANDARD] GAUGE):

No.	Co.	Type	Date	Builder	Length	Weight	Seats	Motors No.	Motors HP	Remarks
2	CIE/GRN	DE DT ArRf Double Deck	1901	Brush	30-0	30,000	67	2	50	from Dublin, Ireland
4	B&K	DE DT DkRf California Style	1900	Holman	26-6	16,000	36	1	25	
51	FTC	DE DT ArRf Center Entrance	1913	St Louis	44-0	40,904	50			body only
83	FTC	DE DT ArRf Birney Safety	1925	St Louis	'42-5	32,920	36			body only, on trucks
88	SDERy	DE DT DkRf California Style	1910	SDERy	40-0	34,100				body only
93	SDERy	DE DT DkRf California Style	1910	SDERy	40-0	34,100				body only
162	SFMRy	DE DT ArRf California Style	1914	Jewett	47-1	48,000	50	4	65	
167	SDERy	DE DT ArRf MU Center Entrance	1914	McG-Cumm	47-8	43,850				body only
171	SFMRy	DE DT ArRf California Style	1923	Bethlehem	47-1	51,000	50	4	65	
179	PE	DE DT ArRf Center Entrance	1912	Pullman						body only; ex-SP 819
316	SDERy	DE ST ArRf Birney Safety	1920	American	28-0	18,200				body only, disassembled
331	PE	DE ST ArRf Birney Safety	1918	Brill	27-9	14,700	32	2	25	
332	PE	DE ST ArRf Birney Safety	1918	Brill	27-9	14,700	32	2	25	
508	SDERy	SE DT ArRf PCC	1936	St Louis	46-10	33,000	62	4	55	

No.	Co.	Type	Date	Builder	Length	Weight	Seats	Motors No.	HP	Remarks
528	SDERy	SE DT ArRf PCC	1938	St Louis	46-10	33,120	62	4	55	
913	NOPSI	DE DT ArRf Closed	1923	P.A. Thomas	47-8	41,148	52	2	65	
1003	SDERy	DE DT ArRf Closed	1913	American						body only; ex-UL&P
1039	SFMRy	SE DT ArRf PCC	1952	St Louis	46-6	37,600	59	4	55	

ELECTRIC SUBURBAN & INTERURBAN CARS (4'8½" [STANDARD] GAUGE):
(Suburban cars are noted as such)

No.	Co.	Type	Date	Builder	Length	Weight	Seats	Motors No.	HP	Remarks
127	BRR	DE DT ArRf Ltwt Interurban	1932	Brill	46-11	42,200	48			body only; ex-FJ&G 127
167	KSTL	DE TT ArRf MU Cent Ent Art. Sub	1937	Bethlehem	110-5	137,625	140	4	105	(two cars perm. joined)
301	VE	DE DT RRRf Trailer Coach	1908	American	49-13/8	50,700	52			body only
302	VE	DE DT RRRf Trailer Coach	1908	American	49-13/8	50,700				body only
314	PE	DE DT ArRf MU Coach	1930	St Louis	72-4	111,000	80	4	140	ex-NWP 384
418	PE	DE DT ArRf MU Coach	1913	Pullman	72-4	125,660	80	4	140	ex-SP 344 (IER)
498	PE	DE DT ArRf MU Baggage-Coach	1913	Pullman	67-81/4	120,000	68	4	140	ex-SP 627 (IER)
511	PE	DE DT RRRf MU Suburban Coach	1901	St Louis	43-0	56,100	48			body only; orig PE 211
538	PE	DE DT RRRf MU Suburban Coach	1909	St Louis	43-05/8	58,500	48	4	50	orig PE 238
717	PE	DE DT ArRf MU Cent Ent Suburban	1925	Brill	52-2	61,700	67	4	65	later PE 5167
1000	PE	DE DT RRRf MU Officer's Car	1913	St Louis	55-61/4	86,800		4	100	body only, on trucks
1001	PE	DE DT RRRf MU Coach	1913	Jewett	55-61/4	84,700	64	4	100	later PE 00199
1225	BCERy	DE DT ArRf MU Coach	1913	St Louis	51-4	70,800	48	4	95	
1440	PE	DE DT ArRf Box Motor	1910	PE	46-2	76,600	—			body only
1498	PE	DE DT RRRf MU Box Motor	1904	St Louis	50-10		—			body only, on trucks; orig PE 881
5112	PE	DE DT ArRf MU Cent Ent Suburban	1922	St Louis	52-2	61,700	65	4	65	orig PE 637
5123	PE	DE DT ArRf MU Cent Ent Suburban	1922	St Louis	52-2	61,700	65	4	65	orig PE 626
5166	PE	DE DT ArRf MU Cent Ent Suburban	1925	Brill	52-2	61,700	65	4	65	orig PE 716

ELECTRIC WORK EQUIPMENT (3'6" [NARROW] GAUGE):

No.	Co.	Type	Date	Builder	Length	Weight	Seats	Motors No.	HP	Remarks
9007	LARy	DE ST ArRf Money Car	1921	American	28-0	17,260				body only, was LARy 1069 (Birney)
9209	LARy	DE DT Motor Flat	1913	LARy	40-1 ½	51,000		4	50	
9225	LATL	DE DT 5-Ton Derrick	1912	LARy	40-0	63,700		4	50	
9310	LATL	DE ST ArRf Rail Grinder	1925	LARy	20-2	25,200		2	50	
9350	LATL	DE DT Tower Car	1907	LARy	30-4	38,600		4	50	
9351	LARy	DE DT Line Const. Car	1907	LARy	36-6	39,720		4	50	
9550	LAMTA	DE ST DkRf Shop Switcher	1904	LARy	12-0	16,780		2	50	
9614	LARy	DE DT Flat Car	1907	LARy	35-9	23,300		—	—	
9615	LATL	DE DT Flat Car	1908	LARy	34-5	23,800		—	—	

ELECTRIC WORK EQUIPMENT (4'8½" [STANDARD] GAUGE):

No.	Co.	Type	Date	Builder	Length	Weight	Seats	Motors No.	HP	Remarks
00150	PE	DT Trolley Wire Greaser	1898	LAP	36-2	33,000	—	4	50	ex-LAP 3
00157	PE	DE DT ArRf Tower Car	1915	PE	48-2	82,000	—	4	100	

TROLLEY COACHES:

No.	Co.	Date	Builder	Remarks
530	SFMRy	1948	M-H	"Baby Marmon"
536	SFMRy	1948	M-H	"Baby Marmon"
614	SFMRy	1949	F-TC	
633	MMS	1940	F-TC	
656	MMS	1944	PStd	
8002	LAMTA	1946	ACF Brill	

ELECTRIC LOCOMOTIVES (4'8½" [STANDARD] GAUGE):

No.	Co.	Wheel Arrgmt	Type	Date	Builder	Weight	HP	Length	Remarks
1	ASARCO	B	Mine Switch Loco	1912	B-W	37,000			250 volt DC
1	H&N	B-B	Locomotive	1921	GE	60,000	260		org. GE demonstrator
653	SN	B-B	MU Locomotive	1928	GE	127,000	1000	35-6	org. SN 1053
1624	PE	B-B	MU Locomotive	1925	PE Ry	125,000	840	38-4	

INTERNAL COMBUSTION LOCOMOTIVES (4'8½" [STANDARD] GAUGE):

No.	Co.	Wheel Arrgmt	Type	Date	Builder	Model	Weight	HP	Length	Remarks
012	DOT	C-C	MU Diesel-Electric	1941	Alco	RS 1 ?	230,000	1000	52-0	ex-USA 8009, ex-TCI 601
015	DOT	C-C	MU Diesel-Electric	1942	Alco	RS 1 ?	230,000	1000	52-0	ex-USA 8018
1	P of LA	B-B	Diesel-Electric	1945	BLW	VO-1000	240,000	1000		ex-USN 65-00249
12	SCE	B	Gas Mech. Switcher	1941	Plymouth	ML-6			22-4	ex-USA
E-60	AP&C	B	Diesel-Electric	1941	GE	B-50/50	50,000	200	16-0	
E-513	AP&C	B	Diesel-Hydraulic	1956	B-L-H	SH-2300-B				
1006	SP	B-B	Diesel-Electric	1939	EMC	SW-1	199,300	600		later Beth. Stl No 15
1474	SP	B-B	Diesel-Electric	1952	Alco	S-4	229,930	1000	41-6	later SP 1802
7441	USAF	B-B	Diesel-Electric	1942	GE		90,000	200		ex-USA 7441
8580	USAF	B-B	MU Diesel-Electric	1944	GE	B-B-90/90	90,000	400		ex-USA 8580

STEAM LOCOMOTIVES (4'8½" [STANDARD] GAUGE):

No.	Co.	Wheel Arrgmt	Type	Date	Builder	Cyl	Weight	T.E.	Length	Remarks
2	MN RR	0-6-0T	Switcher	1917	Davenport	17x24	124,000	23,070	31-9	
2	VC Ry	2-6-2	**Prairie**	1922	Baldwin	18x24	200,070	26,250	57-5	ex-Cascade Lumber 107

STEAM RAILROAD PASSENGER CARS (4'8½" [STANDARD] GAUGE):

No.	Co.	Const.	Type	Date	Builder	Length	Weight	Cap'y	Remarks
Corydon	Pullman	steel	Slpr/7 Cmpt-2 DRm	1917	P. Co.	73-6		20 berths	
20	V&T	wood	Baggage-coach	1908	H.L.&C.				
54	Soo	steel	Business car	1927	Soo Line	79-0	170,760	8 seats	reblt from buffet-bag No. 1704 blt B&S 1914
60	ATSF	steel	Postal car	1924	P.C.&M.	64-3			
122	SP	wood	Business car	1900	A.S.		111,700		
175	SD&AE	steel	Baggage-coach	1915	P.C.&M.	65-8 ¾		24 seats	
204	UP	steel	Rules examiner	1922	P.C.&M.	79-3		24 seats	converted from coach UP 402
542	LA&SL	steel	Chair car	1926	P.C.&M.	78-9		44 seats	modernized 1950
552	D&RGW	wood	Baggage-coach	1891	P.P.C.Co.	59-6		28 seats	
692	OSL	steel	Coach	1911	P.Co.	67-3 ¼	98,700	68 seats	
743	D&RGW	steel	Baggage	1910	B&S.	73-4	131,000	32,000	
745	D&RGW	steel	Baggage	1929	A.C.&F.	73-4	133,000	60,000	ex-D&SL 600
1530	UP	steel	Dormitory-club	1924	P.C.&M.	81-5 1/8		30 seats	
1999	ATSF	steel	Horse Express	1930	P.C.&M.				
2055	ATSF	steel	Baggage-RPO	1930	P.C.&M.	73-1			
2065	UP	steel	Postal car	1914	P.Co.	63-0	121,700		reno. from UP 1267
2419	ATSF	wood	Baggage-coach	1879	Ohio Falls				body only, ex-524
2543	ATSF	steel	Baggage-coach	1911	A.C.&F.	76-10		37 seats	orig M104 (motor car)
2602	ATSF	steel	Baggage-coach	1923	P.Co.	83-11		28 seats	
3010	ATSF	steel	Chair car	1927	P.C.&M.	79-2		72 seats	
3209	ATSF	steel	Parlor car	1910	P.Co.	83-3 ½			orig ATSF 1204
89631	USA	steel	Kitchen car	1953	St Louis				
89647	USA	steel	Kitchen car	1953	St Louis				

FREIGHT CARS (4'8½" [STANDARD] GAUGE):

No.	Co.	Const.	Type	Date	Builder	Length	Weight	Cap'y	Remarks
?	ATSF		Flat			36-0		60,000	
?	T&T	wood	Box	c1885					ex-DL&W 32474, 20450

No.	Co.	Const.	Type	Date	Builder	Length	Weight	Cap'y	Remarks
205	T&T	wood	Flat	1906	S.C.Co.				later US Navy 61-06480
453	GATX	steel	Tank, wine	1930			54,900	87,000	
601	NCC	steel	Side dump	1916	K&J	32-0	59,800		
813	ROX	steel	Tank, oil	1917	N.A.C.Co.		40,100	80,000	
1651	SBIX	sufws	Tank, vinegar	1928	F.T.Co.	36-0	40,300	100,000	
2704	PE	sufws	Box	1924	S.S.C.	40-0	43,400	100,000	later PE 00131, SP MW6258
2721	PE	sufws	Box	1924	S.S.C.	40-0	43,400	100,000	later PE ?, SP MW6259
2729	PE	sufws	Box	1924	S.S.C.	40-0	43,400	100,000	later PE 00117
2731	PE	sufws	Box	1924	S.S.C.	40-0	43,400	100,000	later PE 00118
2737	PE	sufws	Box	1924	S.S.C.	40-0	43,400	100,000	later PE 00119
8875	SFRD	scsws	Refrigerator	1911	A.C.F.	41-3			reno. ATSF 190522 (tool car) 3/18/36
9210	UTLX	steel	Tank, oil	1937	U.T.L.		42,700	80,000	
20305	PFE	steel	Refrigerator	1947	P-Std.	41-0 7/8	52,400	80,000	
21028	SFRD	steel	Refrigerator	1920	A.C.F.	41-5	61,200	75,000	
25840	ATSF	sufcs	Stock		ATSF	40-9	45,100	80,000	underframe from boxcar 118001 blt '23
28504	UP	steel	Gondola	1925	PRSS	51-7	50,700	110,000	
33438	SP	wood	Box-stock	1902	A.C.F.				
43535	PFE	steel	Refrigerator	1937	P-Std.	40-8 1/4	53,100	80,000	
49131	ATSF	scws	Box	1913	P.C.&M.	37-1 1/4		80,000	
56004	UP	steel	Flat	1928	Bettendorf	44-3 1/2	54,600	100,000	later UP 905219
70414	SP	wood	Box	1901	P.P.C.Co.				
70529	GATX	steel	Tank, wine	1941	G.A.T.		55,100	86,000	
73175	SP		Stock	1918	SP				
85727	UP	steel	Hopper	1926	PC&M	34-5	47,800	100,000	
176695	ATSF	sufcs	Gondola	1943					
183206	UP	steel	Box	1936	UP-Omaha	41-9	46,900	100,000	
358835	ASRX	steel	Beet gondola	1955			52,700	110,000	ex-SP 150108 blt 1949 by GATC
61-02479	USN	steel	Box	1942	G.A.T.C.	40-6	47,000	100,000	ex-Naval Supply Depot, Oakland, Calif. No. 4
61-02480	USN	steel	Box	1942	G.A.T.C.	40-6	45,200	100,000	
61-02481	USN	steel	Box	1942	G.A.T.C.	40-6	46,200	100,000	
61-02483	USN	steel	Box	1942	G.A.T.C.	40-6	44,200	100,000	
61-02484	USN	steel	Box	1942	G.A.T.C.	40-6	43,800	100,000	ex-Naval Supply Depot, Oakland, Calif. No. 9
61-02489	USN	steel	Box	1942	G.A.T.C.	40-6	45,300	100,000	
61-02492	USN	steel	Box	1942	G.A.T.C.	40-6	45,100	100,000	
61-02836	USN	steel	Flat	1945		40-9	37,000	100,000	

CABOOSES (4'8½" [STANDARD] GAUGE):

No.	Co.	Const.	Type	Date	Builder	Length	Weight	Cap'y	Remarks
374	SP	steel	Caboose, bay window	1947	A.C.F.				ex-T&NO 500 (?)
570	SP	cufws	Caboose	1924	SP	40-0	42,000		
D-918	ATSF	cufws	Drover's caboose	1929	ATSF		63,900		
1213	SP	steel	Caboose	1942	SP				
1421	ATSF	scswf	Caboose	1923	A.C.F.	35-0	35,000		
1761	ATSF	steel	Caboose	1929	A.C.F.	37-7 3/4	48,600		
1962	PE	sufws	Caboose, flat top	1939	PE	38-0	38,600		
1970	PE	sufws	Caboose	1915	LV ?	39-0	36,900		
1971	PE	sufws	Caboose	c1915	LS&MS	39-0	40,000		
1973	PE	scsws	Caboose	1926	LV	39-0	39,700		
1985	PE	scsws	Caboose	1905	RF&P ?	33-0	35,700		
25129	UP	steel	Caboose	1944	P.C.&M.		54,000		

NON-REVENUE (WORK) EQUIPMENT (4'8½" [STANDARD] GAUGE):

No.	Co.	Const.	Type	Date	Builder	Length	Weight	Cap'y	Remarks
MW 1354	SP	sufws	Supply (box) car				52,400		ex-SP 20451
MW 7090	SP	steel	Wrecking derrick	1912	Ind. Wks.	26-2 1/2	222,100		
MW 7091	SP	steel	Relief tender	1912	SP	53-0	136,800		
189783	ATSF	steel	Fuel & water car	1939	ATSF		60,400		underframe from boxcar 34591
190548	ATSF	sufws	Wheel car	1947	ATSF				underframe from boxcar 62032
193673	ATSF	cufws	Foreman's car	1932	ATSF		50,000		
199774	ATSF	steel	Wrecking derrick	1909	Ind. Wks.	26-2 1/2	240,800		missing mechanism

Items which are blank in this roster are either unknown or not currently installed on the vehicle.

ABBREVIATIONS

Operators ("Co." column in tables)

ASRX	Spreckels Sugar Division, American Sugar & Refining (AMSTAR) Co.
AP&C	American Potash & Chemical
ASARCO	American Smelting & Refining Co.
ATSF	Atchison, Topeka & Santa Fe Railway
B&K	Bakersfield & Kern Electric Railway Co.
BRR	Bamberger Railroad
BethStl	Bethlehem Steel Co.
BCERy	British Columbia Electric Railway
CIE	Coras Iompar Eireann (Transportation Authority of the Republic of Ireland)
CSCRR	California Street Cable Railroad Co.
DL&W	Delaware, Lackawanna & Western Railroad
DOT	United States Department of Transportation
D&RGW	Denver & Rio Grande Western Railroad
D&SL	Denver & Salt Lake Railroad
FJ&G	Fonda, Johnstown & Gloversville
FTC	Fresno Traction Co.
GATX	General American Tank Co. (pre-c.1930)
	General American Transportation Co. (post-c.1930)
G&M	Glendale & Montrose Railway
GRN	Great Northern Railway, Ireland
HBL	Harbor Belt Line Railroad
H&N	Hutchinson & Northern Railway
IER	Interurban Electric Railway (former Oakland, Alameda & Berkeley Lines of the SP)
KSTL	Key System Transit Lines
Kyoto	Kyoto City Transit Lines (?), Japan
LAJ	Los Angeles Junction Railway Co.
LAP	Los Angeles Pacific (a predecessor to PE)
LARy	Los Angeles Railway Co. (1895-1945)
LATL	Los Angeles Transit Lines (1945-1958)
LAMTA	Los Angeles Metropolitan Transit Authority (1958-1963)
LA&SL	Los Angeles & Salt Lake Railroad
LS&MS	Lake Shore & Michigan Southern Railroad
LV	Lehigh Valley Railroad
MNRR	Mojave Northern Railroad
MMS	Municipality of Metropolitan Seattle
NCC	New Cornelia Copper Co.
NOPSI	New Orleans Public Service, Inc.
NWP	Northwestern Pacific Railroad
OSL	Oregon Short Line
PCRR	Pacific Coast Railroad
PE	Pacific Electric Railway Co.
PFE	Pacific Fruit Express (owned jointly by Southern Pacific Co. and Union Pacific R.R. 1906-1978)
PofLA	Port of Los Angeles
Pullman	The Pullman Co. (1899-1927)
	Pullman, Inc. (1927-1947)
	The Pullman Co. (1947-1968)
ROX	Richfield Oil Co.
SBIX	Standard Brands, Inc.
SCE	Southern California Edison Co.
SD&AE	San Diego & Arizona Eastern Railway
SDERy	San Diego Electric Railway Co.
SFMRy	San Francisco Municipal Railway
SFRD	Santa Fe Refrigerator Dispatch (owned by AT&SF Ry. 1884—c.1984)
Soo	Minneapolis, St. Paul & Sault Ste. Marie Railroad (Soo Line)
SN	Sacramento Northern Railway
SP	Southern Pacific Co. (c. 1869-1970)
	Southern Pacific Transportation Co. (1970-present)
TC&I	Tennessee Coal & Iron
T&NO	Texas & New Orleans
TC&GB	Tucson, Cornelia & Gila Bend Railroad
T&T	Tonopah & Tidewater Railroad
UL&P	Utah Light & Power
UP	Union Pacific Railroad Co.
USAF	United States Air Force

USA	United States Army
USN	United States Navy
UTLX	Union Tank Car Co.
VCRy	Ventura County Railway Co.
VE	Visalia Electric Railway Co.
V&T	Virginia & Truckee Railway
YVT	Yakima Valley Transportation Co.

Type

DE	Double Ended; capable of being operated from both ends
SE	Single Ended; capable of regular operation in only one direction
DT	Double Truck; equipped with two trucks or wheelsets, each independently sprung and equalized, freely movable under carbody
ST	Single Truck; equipped with a single wheelset rigidly attached to carbody
TT	Three Truck; equipped with three independently sprung trucks or wheelsets, carbody (articulated, actually two separate cars) shares middle wheelset in order to bend in middle
ArRf	Arch Roof; see diagram following
BbRf	Bombay Roof; see diagram following
DkRf	Deck Roof; see diagram following
RfRf	Railroad Roof; see diagram following

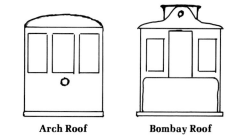 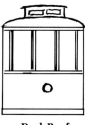 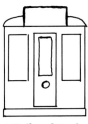

Arch Roof   **Bombay Roof**   **Deck Roof**   **Railroad Roof**

Wheel Arrangement

B	One single, rigidly attached four-wheel (two axle) truck or wheelset
B-B	Two freely movable, independently sprung and equalized, four-wheel (two axle) trucks or wheelsets
C-C	Two freely movable, independently sprung and equalized, six-wheel (three axle) trucks or wheelsets
0-6-0T	No leading wheels, six main drivers, no trailing wheels, with the water and fuel oil tanks mounted right on the engine
2-6-2	Two leading wheels, six main drivers, two trailing wheels, with a separate fuel and water tender

Construction

sufws	Steel Underframe, Wooden Superstructure
sufcs	Steel Underframe, Composite (wood and steel) Superstructure
scsws	Steel Centersill, Wooden Superstructure

The typeface used in this book is Dominante, set the old-fashioned way, on a linotype, by Ray Ballash. Captions and headings are in Melior, set by Lori Clarke/Franklin Press and Roc-Pacific Typographics.

Color Separations: Quadcolor, Burbank, California

Printing: G.R. Huttner Litho, Burbank, California

Book Design and Layout by Paul Hammond

Just like a street scene of old, it's an unhurried day at the museum as the evening shadows lengthen on Broadway in front of Carbarn #1. The photographer was Ken Kemzura.